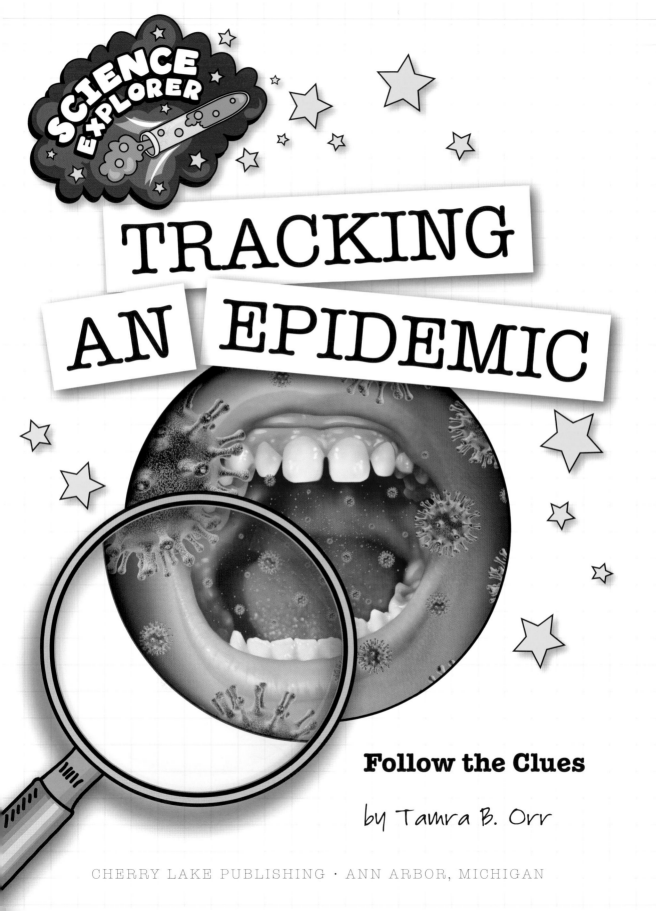

SCIENCE EXPLORER

TRACKING AN EPIDEMIC

Follow the Clues

by Tamra B. Orr

CHERRY LAKE PUBLISHING · ANN ARBOR, MICHIGAN

CHERRY LAKE Publishing

Published in the United States of America by Cherry Lake Publishing
Ann Arbor, Michigan
www.cherrylakepublishing.com

CONTENT EDITOR: Robert Wolffe, EdD, Professor of Teacher Education, Bradley University, Peoria, Illinois
BOOK DESIGN AND ILLUSTRATION: The Design Lab
READING ADVISER: Marla Conn, ReadAbility, Inc.

PHOTO CREDITS: Cover and page 1, © Lightspring/Shutterstock, Inc.; page 4, © Tom Wang/Shutterstock, Inc.; page 5, © anyaivanova/Shutterstock, Inc.; page 6, © Joseph/Shutterstock, Inc.; page 7, © Kamira/Shutterstock, Inc.; page 8, ©Everett Collection Historical/Alamy; page 9, © Daria Filimonova/Shutterstock, Inc.; page 10, © Medical-on-Line / Alamy; page 11, © Nick Gregory / Alamy; page 12, © Goekce Narttek/Shutterstock, Inc.; page 13, © Darren Baker/Shutterstock, Inc.; page 14, © PhotoSky/Shutterstock, Inc.; page 15, © Tyler Olson/Shutterstock, Inc.; page 16, © lightwavemedia/Shutterstock, Inc.; page 17, © Lisa S./Shutterstock, Inc.; page 18, © Andrey Arkusha/Shutterstock, Inc.; page 19, © Ralf Maassen (DTEurope)/Shutterstock, Inc.; page 20, © Panom Pensawang/Shutterstock, Inc.; page 21, © Guzel Studio/Shutterstock, Inc.; pages 22, 26, and 27, © Ermolaev Alexander/Shutterstock, Inc.; page 23, © Blend Images / Alamy; page 24, © Blend Images / Alamy; page 25, © wavebreakmedia/Shutterstock, Inc.; page 28, © Jenn Huls/Shutterstock, Inc.; page 29, © kavida/Shutterstock, Inc.

LIBRARY OF CONGRESS CATALOGING-IN-PUBLICATION DATA
Orr, Tamra, author.
Tracking an epidemic / by Tamra B. Orr.
pages cm. — (Science explorer) (Follow the clues)
Summary: "Follow along with Abigail as she learns about epidemiology using the scientific method."— Provided by publisher.
Audience: Grades 4 to 6.
Includes bibliographical references and index.
ISBN 978-1-62431-776-7 (lib. bdg.) — ISBN 978-1-62431-786-6 (pbk.) —
ISBN 978-1-62431-806-1 (ebook) — ISBN 978-1-62431-796-5 (pdf) 1. Epidemics—
Juvenile literature. 2. Communicable diseases—Juvenile literature. I. Title. II. Series.

Cherry Lake Publishing would like to acknowledge
the work of The Partnership for 21st Century Skills.
Please visit www.p21.org for more information.

Printed in the United States of America, Corporate Graphics Inc.
January 2014

TABLE OF CONTENTS

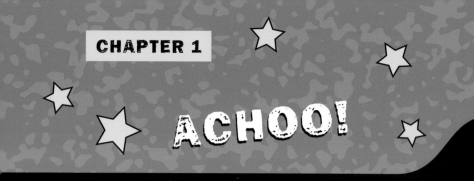

CHAPTER 1

ACHOO!

⤷ An illness such as the flu can spread quickly and easily.

Abigail grabbed a tissue just in time to get it in front of her face before sneezing yet again. Being sick was absolutely no fun. She had spent the day in bed, but she still felt tired. Abby had the flu, just like her father and her brother, Alex, had gotten last week. In fact, almost everyone Abby knew either had just gotten over the flu or was in the middle of it like she was. So many students and teachers were sick that school had closed for a few days. Abby's mom said the city had a flu **epidemic**!

Abby's mom worked as an **epidemiologist**, but Abby called her a disease detective. It was Mrs. Stockton's job to watch for clues—like sneezes, fevers, aches, and pains—and figure out what disease was the villain. Instead of making people feel better like a medical doctor would, Mrs. Stockton spent her time tracking down where the illness started and figuring out how it could be stopped before it spread farther.

It wasn't an easy job, but it was a fascinating one. Abby had watched her mom conduct dozens of interviews, travel to other cities, and spend hours in the lab trying to put clues together. Just then, Abby sneezed again. While her mom's job was hard, Abby almost envied her. Anything had to be better than having the flu!

Epidemiologists try to understand how a disease works.

Mrs. Stockton knocked lightly on Abby's bedroom door. "Feeling any better?" she asked.

"Not really," Abby replied. "All this sneezing is awful!"

"Well, you aren't alone," Mrs. Stockton said. "It seems like everybody in town has caught this bug."

"Ugh," said Abby as she reached for another tissue. She blew her nose, then suddenly had an idea. "Mom, where do you think this disease came from?"

The flu may feel like a common cold at first, but the flu worsens much more quickly.

Feeling the temperature of someone's forehead can help determine if she has a fever.

"I'm not sure," Mrs. Stockton responded.

"Well, it had to come from somewhere, right?" Abby asked.

"Indeed it did," said Mrs. Stockton as she knelt down to feel the temperature of Abby's forehead. "Are you wondering who's to blame for the miserable time you're having?"

"Yeah!" Abby answered, coughing lightly as she spoke. "Can we try to figure it out? Isn't that what your job is all about?"

"We can sure give it a try," said Mrs. Stockton. "I suppose I wouldn't mind knowing the answer myself!"

A DEADLY OUTBREAK

A school gym being used as a flu ward, filled with Spanish flu patients.

Sometimes an epidemic becomes an even bigger problem. When a deadly disease spreads quickly over a large area, the **outbreak** is known as a **pandemic**. Pandemics are major global health crises, and they can kill huge numbers of people if they are not contained quickly. One of the most devastating pandemics of all time occurred in 1918 and 1919, when a new type of flu **infected** troops at a military base in Kansas during World War I. When these soldiers traveled overseas to fight in the war, they brought the sickness with them and made many people in Europe sick. As the newly infected people traveled, the disease eventually spread to almost every part of the world. Doctors were unable to keep such a widespread pandemic under control, and somewhere between 25 million and 50 million people died during the outbreak.

CHAPTER 2

A SPREADING SICKNESS

↰ Hot tea can help ease a cough and soothe a sore throat.

Abby and Mrs. Stockton sat at the kitchen table, each with a mug of steaming hot tea. Abby was wrapped in her favorite blanket.

"Are you sure you feel well enough to be out of bed?" asked Mrs. Stockton. "You don't look so good."

"I'm okay," Abby replied as she slowly sipped her tea. "I'll feel even better once we get to the bottom of this mystery."

"That's the spirit!" Mrs. Stockton said, chuckling.

"So how does one sickness spread to so many people anyway?" asked Abby. "Almost everyone I know has had the flu lately, even people who've never met each other. It seems almost impossible!"

"It's not impossible at all," Mrs. Stockton answered. "In fact, it happens all the time. When a group of people in one area all come down with the same illness, it is called an epidemic."

"That makes sense," said Abby, "but where does it start? And how does it spread to so many people so quickly?"

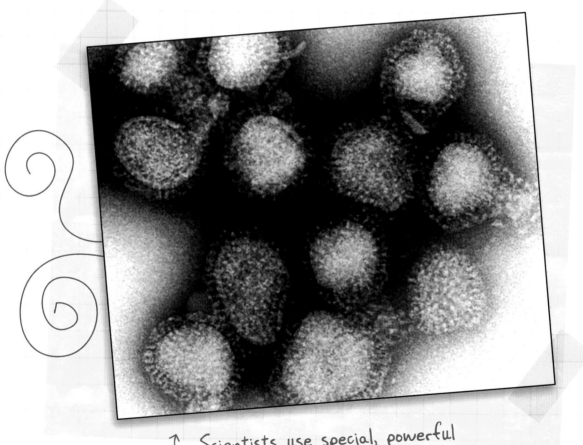

↖ Scientists use special, powerful microscopes to see flu viruses.

↖ Covering your mouth when you sneeze or cough helps contain a virus.

"The sickness going through our town is caused by a **virus** called influenza," Mrs. Stockton explained. "Viruses are extremely tiny particles that infect our bodies and make us feel sick. Once one person gets sick, the virus can easily spread to a larger group. Different viruses spread in different ways, but the flu is mostly spread when infected people cough and sneeze. The virus particles shoot out into the air, and then other people breathe them in."

"So you're saying that this whole epidemic started with just one person?" Abby asked.

"Probably, yes," said Mrs. Stockton.

A traveler can carry a disease from one place to another.

"Hmm," said Abby. "But how did that person get sick in the first place?"

"It can happen in a few different ways," Mrs. Stockton replied. "Certain epidemics can be spread by animals, the water, or the soil. With a sickness such as the flu, sometimes a new form of the illness forms inside someone's body. It makes the person sick and begins spreading through the air. Other times, a person goes where there are sick people, gets infected, and then brings the virus back home."

"Yikes," said Abby. "So how are we going to figure out who started this mess?"

"We can use the scientific method," Mrs. Stockton said. "It is a process we can use to study the world and solve problems scientifically." She wrote a few lines on a piece of paper and passed it across the table for Abby to see. "Here are the steps."

The scientific method can be applied to epidemiology, as well as many other sciences.

THE SCIENTIFIC METHOD
1. Ask a question
2. Gather information and observe/research
3. Make a **hypothesis**—or guess the answer
4. Experiment to test your hypothesis
5. Analyze your test results
6. Present a conclusion

"We have a question already," said Mrs. Stockton.

"'Who started this epidemic?' right?" Abby asked.

"Exactly," Mrs. Stockton replied. "And I just gave you some information about viruses and how the flu spreads from person to person. So the next step is to form a hypothesis. In other words, you can use what you know to make a guess about how the epidemic started."

Abby wrinkled her brow as she thought about what she had learned about the flu. "Well, it seems like most of the people who got sick go to my school or know someone who does. I bet that if we look into it, we might find out that someone at school went on a trip recently," she said.

"An excellent hypothesis!" Mrs. Stockton said. "Now we can investigate to see if it's correct!"

Scientists often learn as much as they can about a topic in order to make an informed hypothesis.

FINDING PATIENT ZERO

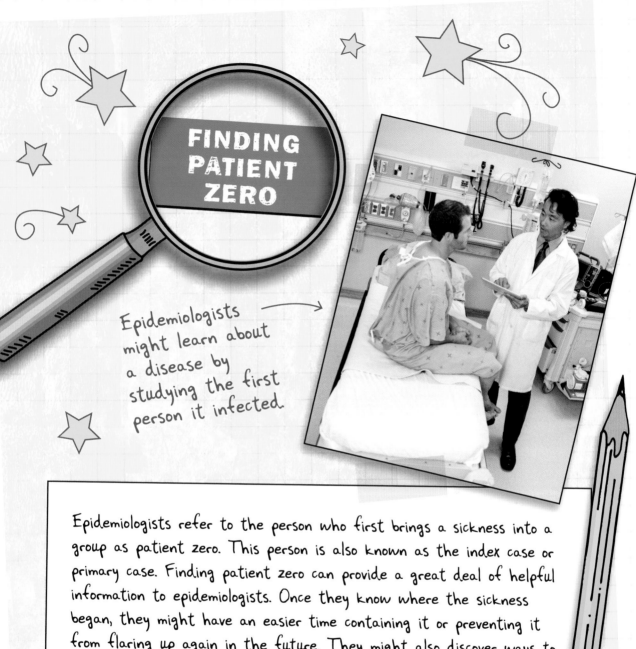

Epidemiologists might learn about a disease by studying the first person it infected.

Epidemiologists refer to the person who first brings a sickness into a group as patient zero. This person is also known as the index case or primary case. Finding patient zero can provide a great deal of helpful information to epidemiologists. Once they know where the sickness began, they might have an easier time containing it or preventing it from flaring up again in the future. They might also discover ways to treat the disease more effectively. Because some viruses can cause major health problems or even kill infected people, epidemiologists work hard to find answers as quickly as possible during an epidemic.

CHAPTER 3

TRACKING THE OUTBREAK

Epidemiologists often have huge amounts of data to record.

"Okay," said Mrs. Stockton. "To figure out where this epidemic started we can make a record of everyone who has gotten the flu so far. We can also note when they got the flu and ask them if they have traveled anywhere recently." She opened up her laptop computer and began typing.

"What are you doing?" asked Abby.

"I'm making a chart so we can keep track of all the patients' infor-mation," Mrs. Stockton answered. After a moment, she finished typing and turned the screen around so Abby could see. "See, I've entered the information for you, your dad, and your brother."

Name	Infection Date	Recently Traveled?	Travel Dates
Abby	11/14/2013	No	–
Alex	11/6/2013	No	–
Dad	11/5/2013	Yes	11/1/2013 to 11/3/2013

Patients can answer questions on where they have been, whom they have been with, and other information to help epidemiologists.

"I forgot about dad's business trip," said Abby. "Do you think he brought the flu to the area?"

"I'm pretty sure there were other people already sick before him," Mrs. Stockton answered. "The only way to find out for sure is to start gathering more information, though."

"So many people got sick!" Abby exclaimed. "Where do we even start?"

"Let's start with the people we know about," Mrs. Stockton answered. "Because our hypothesis is that the illness started with someone in your school, it is a good place to begin. We can call students and teachers on the phone and ask them when they started feeling ill. We can also ask them if they know of any other people who got sick."

"Awesome," said Abby. She stood up to go get the phone book sent home by the school. "Let's get started!"

↑ Abby and Mrs. Stockton's questions could easily be answered over the telephone.

COMPUTER VIRUS

People often tweet or post on the Internet when they're sick.

Epidemiologists and other health professionals are always looking for better ways of gathering information about sicknesses. When a flu epidemic broke out in the United States in December 2012, scientists kept track of its spread using a revolutionary new method. Computer scientists at Johns Hopkins University in Baltimore, Maryland, created a computer program that scanned postings on the social media service Twitter. They wanted to see who was talking about having the flu and where these people were located. This allowed researchers to track the flu's movements very closely. In the future, similar systems could be used to track epidemics of all kinds.

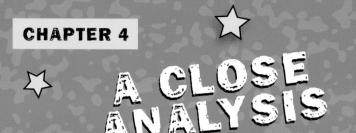

CHAPTER 4

A CLOSE ANALYSIS

↳ Abby and Mrs. Stockton had to call a lot of people because the flu had spread very quickly.

"Whew!" said Abby as she hung up the phone. "That was a lot of calling, but I think we finally got everyone I can think of."

"Excellent," said Mrs. Stockton. "We have a lot of information in our chart. Now it is time to take a closer look and analyze the data. We'll see what we can figure out about this epidemic that we didn't already know."

"We talked to so many people that I don't even know where to begin," Abby said. "What should we do?"

"Well," Mrs. Stockton began, "with a couple of clicks, we can easily reorganize our chart—"

"By the infection date!" Abby finished her mother's thought. "Then we can see who were the first people to get sick."

"Exactly," said Mrs. Stockton, clicking on the laptop's track pad. "Here we go. Take a look, Abby. Here are the first people to get sick."

Name	Infection Date	Recently Traveled?	Travel Dates
Steve L.	10/30/2013	No	—
Sara W.	10/30/2013	No	—
Ms. Jackson	10/30/2013	Yes	10/26/2013 to 10/28/2013
Tim L.	10/30/2013	No	—
Neil F.	10/30/2013	Yes	10/16/2013 to 10/21/2013

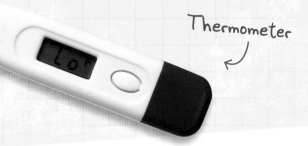

Thermometer

"Look Mom. All five people on the list got sick on the same day," Abby noticed.

"Keep in mind that that is just the first day they noticed the **symptoms**," Mrs. Stockton pointed out. "Sometimes people are infected for one to three days before feeling sick. Are there any other connections between these people?"

Abby looked at the chart and thought hard for a moment. Suddenly, she remembered something. "They're all in the same class!"

"Really?" asked Mrs. Stockton. "That is a very useful thing to know."

Abby noticed that the epidemic started with people in the same class.

The flu can spread rapidly among students and teachers in a school.

"I'm friends with Neil, and Ms. Jackson is his homeroom teacher," Abby said. "Steve, Sara, and Tim are all in that class, too."

"Notice anything else?" Mrs. Stockton asked.

"Neil and Ms. Jackson are the only ones who traveled recently or had someone in their family who traveled.," Abby said. "But how will we know which one of them spread the virus? Should we ask them more questions?"

Mrs. Stockton smiled as she got up to pour fresh mugs of tea. "We actually have all the information we need right here. Remember everything I told you, and see if you can figure it out."

EVERYDAY EPIDEMIOLOGY

Epidemiologists look for better ways to treat and prevent outbreaks.

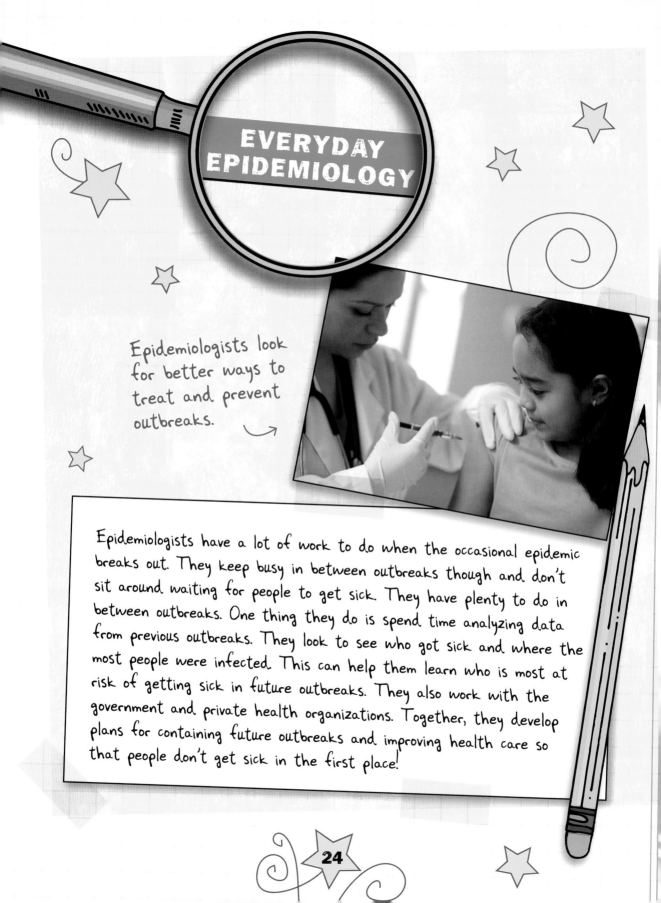

Epidemiologists have a lot of work to do when the occasional epidemic breaks out. They keep busy in between outbreaks though and don't sit around waiting for people to get sick. They have plenty to do in between outbreaks. One thing they do is spend time analyzing data from previous outbreaks. They look to see who got sick and where the most people were infected. This can help them learn who is most at risk of getting sick in future outbreaks. They also work with the government and private health organizations. Together, they develop plans for containing future outbreaks and improving health care so that people don't get sick in the first place!

CHAPTER 5

SOLVING THE PUZZLE

It can be exciting to put all the data together and find the answer you've been looking for.

Abby was smiling wide as her mom sat back down at the table. "Wow," said Mrs. Stockton. "You're looking much healthier than you were earlier this afternoon."

"I feel a lot better now that I've solved this mystery," said Abby.

Mrs. Stockton smiled and took a sip of her tea. "Are you ready to present your conclusion?"

"I sure am," said Abby. "I looked at the data and thought about everything you taught me about the flu virus."

"And?" Mrs. Stockton asked, raising her eyebrows.

"It was Ms. Jackson!" Abby replied. "It had to be her."

"That's what I thought, too," said Mrs. Stockton. "I see you must have taken a close look at the dates when she and Neil were traveling."

"Exactly," Abby responded. "Once I thought about it, I realized that it couldn't have been Neil. He got back from his trip on October 21, but he

↑ Neil had been back in school for too long before the outbreak to have been the source.

A person with the flu can be contagious before he or she even feels symptoms.

didn't get sick until nine days later. You told me that some people can have the flu virus for up to three days before getting sick. So Neil would have had to show symptoms earlier for it to have been him."

"Good thinking," Mrs. Stockton said. "It is also helpful to know that people are usually only **contagious** for about a week after they are infected. With Ms. Jackson coming back to school just a couple of days before everyone got sick, it is much more likely that she was our patient zero."

"Whew," Abby said. "All this investigating has tired me out."

↳ The flu can make a person very tired. It is important to get plenty of rest!

"I'm surprised you didn't get tired earlier," said Mrs. Stockton. "You do still have the flu, after all. How about you head back to bed, and I'll wake you up at dinnertime?"

Abby laid down in her bed and snuggled up in her covers. She thought about how much fun she had had that day, even though she was sick. Being an epidemiologist seemed like a really great job. "Achoo!" Abby sneezed, covering her face just in the nick of time. She couldn't wait to help her mom solve more mysteries—that is, as soon as she was feeling better!

UNDER CONTROL

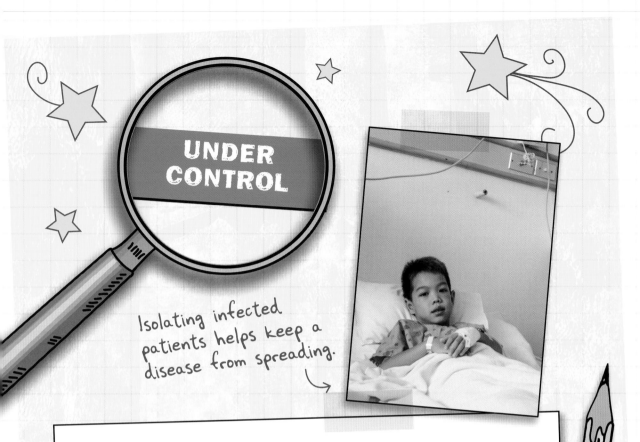

Isolating infected patients helps keep a disease from spreading.

When an epidemic breaks out, epidemiologists join forces with other health officials and fly into action. The first thing they do is test patients to confirm the identity of the sickness. Then they work to prevent the sickness from spreading farther. They can do this by educating the community about the outbreak, encouraging people to avoid places where they might get sick, and **isolating** infected patients. They also collect information to try to determine the outbreak's origin. This can help them figure out who is most at risk of being infected. Depending on the sickness, epidemiologists and other experts might distribute **vaccines** or other preventive medications to people who haven't been infected yet. With a lot of hard work and a little luck, they will prevent the outbreak from becoming a major problem.

GLOSSARY

contagious (kuhn-TAY-juhs) able to spread a disease

epidemic (ep-i-DEM-ik) an infectious disease present in a large number of people at the same time

epidemiologist (ep-uh-dee-mee-AH-luh-jist) someone who studies the causes of sicknesses

hypothesis (hye-PAH-thi-sis) an idea that could explain how something works but must be proven by the scientific method

infected (in-FEKT-id) caused disease or contaminated by introducing germs or viruses

isolating (EYE-suh-lay-ting) keeping something or someone alone or separate

outbreak (OUT-brake) the sudden start of something unpleasant

pandemic (pan-DEM-ik) an outbreak of a disease that affects a very large region or the whole world

symptoms (SIMP-tuhmz) signs of an illness

vaccines (vack-SEENZ) substances containing dead, weakened, or living organisms that can be injected or taken orally; a vaccine causes a person to produce antibodies that protect him or her from the disease caused by the organisms

virus (VYE-ruhs) a very tiny organism that can reproduce and grow only when inside living cells; viruses cause diseases such as polio, measles, the common cold, and AIDS

FOR MORE INFORMATION

BOOKS

Keyser, Amber. *Anatomy of a Pandemic*. Mankato, Minn.: Capstone Press, 2011.

Marciniak, Kristin. *The Flu Pandemic of 1918*. Minneapolis: ABDO Publishing, 2013.

Yomtov, Nel. *Epidemiologist*. Ann Arbor, MI: Cherry Lake Publishing, 2013.

WEB SITES

KidsHealth: Stop the Spread

http://kidshealth.org/kid/h1n1_center/flu_spread.html

Learn how to avoid catching the flu.

National Institute of Environmental Health Sciences:

Epidemiology . . . What is That?

http://kids.niehs.nih.gov/explore/scienceworks/epidemiology.htm

Find out more about what epidemiologists do.

INDEX

ABOUT THE AUTHOR

Tamra B. Orr is an author living in the Pacific Northwest. Orr has a degree in Secondary Education and English from Ball State University. She is the mother to four, and the author of more than 350 books for readers of all ages. When she isn't writing or reading books, she is writing letters to friends all over the world Although fascinated by all aspects of science, most of her current scientific method skills are put to use tracking down lost socks, missing keys, and overdue library books.